W9-BUK-342

ABOUT THE BOOK

This well-known folk song by Oscar Brand is enthusiastically and vigorously illustrated by Doris Burn in this rollicking presentation of the American pioneer.

In the humorous narrative, the settler clears the land for his farm and builds a shack called "Break my Back." But as the verses grow longer, there's a cow who won't give milk, a horse who won't work, and other problems. Still he remains optimistic and says after each episode:

But the land was sweet and good
And I did what I could.

A rhyming, cumulative text with down-to-earth, funny illustrations, this picture book is bound to be a favorite.

WHEN I FIRST CAME TO THIS LAND

by OSCAR BRAND
PICTURES BY DORIS BURN

G. P. PUTNAM'S SONS • NEW YORK

Second Impression

Words and music by Oscar Brand
 Published simultaneously in
Canada by Longman Canada Limited, Toronto.
SBN: GB-399-60906-7 SBN: TR-399-20415-6
Library of Congress Catalog Card Number: 74-77596
PRINTED IN THE UNITED STATES OF AMERICA
04208

WHEN I FIRST CAME TO THIS LAND

When I first came to this land
I was not a wealthy man.

So I got myself a farm
And I did what I could.
Called my farm
"Power in the Arm"

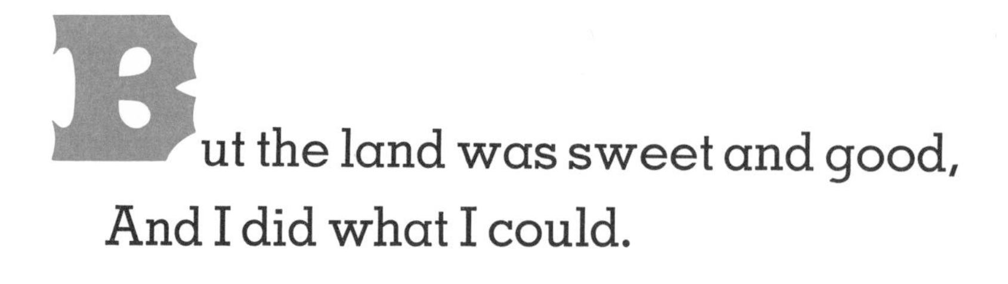

But the land was sweet and good,
And I did what I could.

When I first came to this land
I was not a wealthy man.
So I built myself a shack
And I did what I could.
Called my shack
"Break my Back"

Called my farm
"Power in the Arm"

But the land was sweet and good,
And I did what I could.

When I first came to this land
I was not a wealthy man.
So I got myself a horse
And I did what I could.
Called my horse
"Tired, of Course"

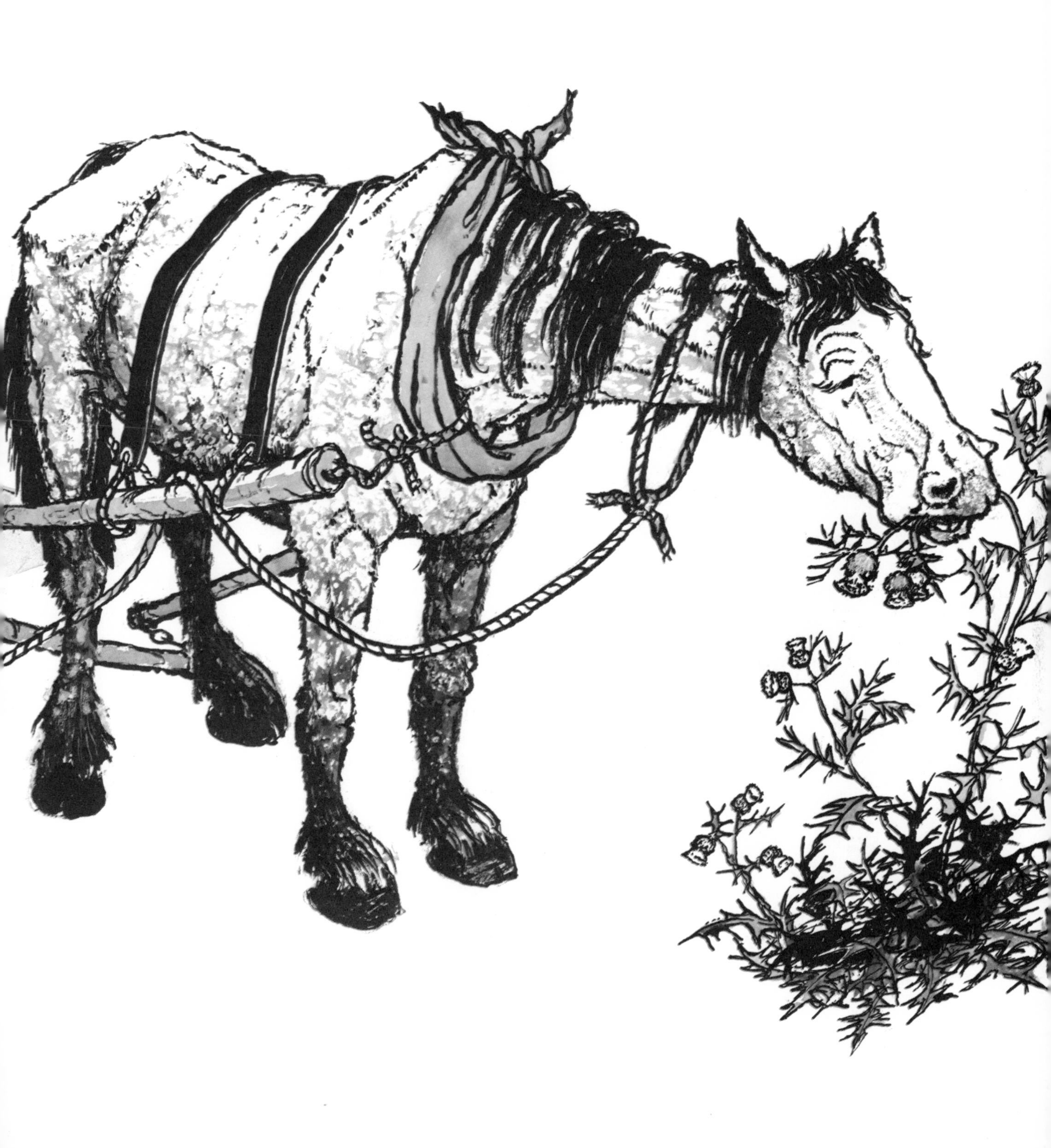

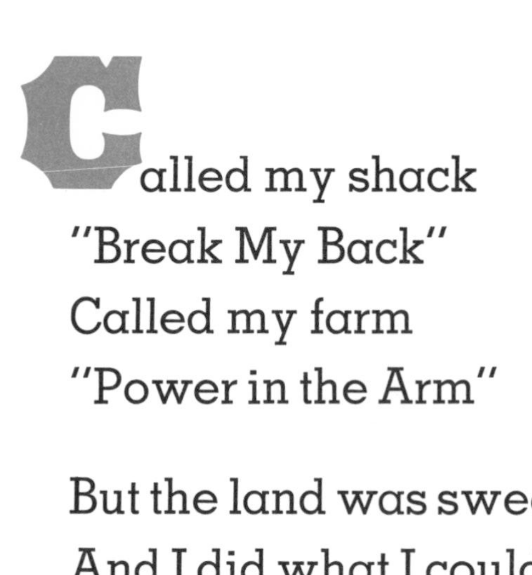

Called my shack
"Break My Back"
Called my farm
"Power in the Arm"

But the land was sweet and good,
And I did what I could.

When I first came to this land
I was not a wealthy man.
So I got myself a cow
And I did what I could.
Called my cow
"No Milk Now"

Called my horse
"Tired, of Course"
Called my shack
"Break My Back"
Called my farm
"Power in the Arm"

But the land was sweet and good,
And I did what I could.

When I first came to this land
I was not a wealthy man.
So I got myself a duck
And I did what I could.
Called my duck
"Out of Luck"

Called my cow
"No Milk Now"
Called my horse
"Tired, of Course"
Called my shack
"Break My Back"

Called my farm
"Power in the Arm"
But the land was sweet and good,
And I did what I could.

When I first came to this land
I was not a wealthy man.
So I got myself a pig
And I did what I could.
Called my pig
"Too Darned Big"

Called my duck
"Out of Luck"
Called my cow
"No Milk Now"
Called my horse
"Tired, of Course"

Called my shack
"Break My Back"
Called my farm
"Power in the Arm"
But the land was sweet and good,
And I did what I could.

When I first came to this land
I was not a wealthy man.
So I got myself a wife
And I did what I could.
Called my wife
"Love of My Life"

Called my pig
"Too Darned Big"
Called my duck
"Out of Luck"

Called my cow
"No Milk Now"
Called my horse
"Tired, of Course"
Called my shack
"Break My Back"

Called my farm
"Power in the Arm"
But the land was sweet and good,
And I did what I could.

When I first came to this land
I was not a wealthy man.
So I got myself a son,
And I did what I could.
Told my son
"My Work's Done"

Called my wife
"Love of My Life"

Called my pig
"Too Darned Big"

Called my duck
"Out of Luck"

Called my cow
"No Milk Now"

Called my horse
"Tired, of Course"

Called my shack
"Break My Back"
Called my farm
"Power in the Arm"

But the land was sweet and good,
And I'd done what I could.

When I First Came To This Land

Words and Music by
OSCAR BRAND
Simply
D G D G D A7 D
1. When I first came to this land, I was not a wealth - y man. Then I built my - self a shack, I did what I could.
2. When I first came to this land, I was not a wealth - y man. Then I bought my - self a cow, I did what I could.
3. When I first came to this land, I was not a wealth - y man. Then I bought my - self a horse, I did what I could.
4. When I first came to this land, I was not a wealth - y man. Then I bought my - self a duck, I did what I could.
G D G D A7 D G D
Fine
mf
mp
Fine

When I First Came To This Land

Words and Music by
OSCAR BRAND
Simply
mf
mp
D G D G D A7 D
1. When I first came to this land, I was not a wealth - y man. Then I
2. When I first came to this land, I was not a wealth - y man. Then I
3. When I first came to this land, I was not a wealth - y man. Then I
4. When I first came to this land, I was not a wealth - y man. Then I
G D G D A7 D G D
built my - self a shack, I did what I could.
bought my - self a cow, I did what I could.
bought my - self a horse, I did what I could.
bought my - self a duck, I did what I could.
Fine
Fine

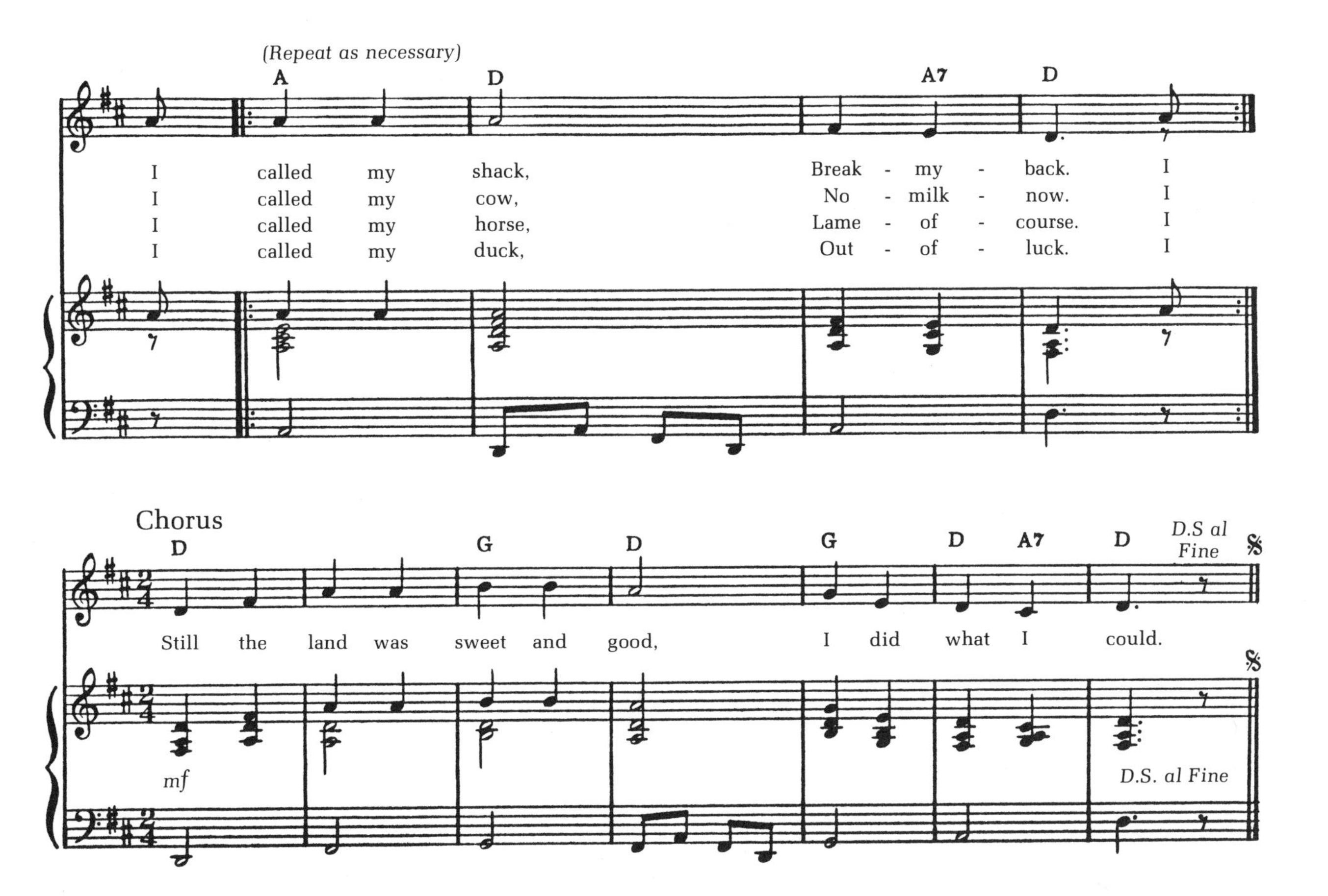
(Repeat as necessary)
A
D
A7
D
I called my shack, Break - my - back. I
I called my cow, No - milk - now. I
I called my horse, Lame - of - course. I
I called my duck, Out - of - luck. I
Chorus
D
G
D
G
D
A7
D
D.S al Fine
Still the land was sweet and good, I did what I could.
mf
D.S. al Fine

5. When I first came to this land, I was not a wealthy man.
 Then I got myself a wife. I did what I could.
 I called my wife, Love - of - my - life,
 I called my duck, Out - of - luck,
 I called my horse, Tired - of - course,
 I called my cow, No - milk - now,
 I called my shack, Break - my - back.

 CHORUS

6. When I first came to this land, I was not a wealthy man.
 Then I got myself a son, I did what I could.
 I told my son: "My work's done".

 CHORUS: For the land was sweet and good,
 I did what I could.

THE AUTHOR

For a performance at the Town Hall in 1948, OSCAR BRAND was asked to write a song about immigrants coming to this country. He was to describe their struggles in developing the land and the happiness they found: and so he composed "When I First Came to This Land". Since that performance the song has traveled across the country, spreading in fame.

Oscar Brand has written several books of music, recorded fifty-five LP's, and has written and composed hundreds of songs. This well-known folk-singer is on the faculty of Hofstra University and the New School for Social Research. He lives with his family in Great Neck, New York.

THE ARTIST

DORIS BURN had always wanted to live on an island. She attended the universities of Oregon, Hawaii, and Washington, where she received her degree, before she found an island home on Waldron in Washington. She now lives in Seattle, Washington, and spends summers on the island.

She has written and illustrated two books for children: *Andrew Henry's Meadow* and *The Summerfolk,* and illustrated *We Were Tired of Living in a House.*